Somewhere Near In The Dark

Rachael M Nicholas
Somewhere Near In The Dark

20/20 **EYEWEAR**
PAMPHLET SERIES
2014

First published in 2014 by Eyewear Publishing Ltd
74 Leith Mansions, Grantully Road
London W9 1LJ United Kingdom

Typeset with graphic design by Edwin Smet
Author photograph by Rachael M Nicholas
Printed in England by Lightning Source
All rights reserved © 2014 *Rachael M Nicholas*
The right of Rachael M Nicholas to be identified as author of this work
has been asserted in accordance with section 77 of the Copyright,
Designs and Patents Act 1988

ISBN 978-1-908998-62-0
WWW.EYEWEARPUBLISHING.COM

Thanks to
my family, to my friends,
and to Les Robinson and Luke Kennard.

To my family, Natalie, and Suzanna first of all.

Table of contents

9 *Undarling*
11 *An arc, and etc*
13 *Versus*
15 *Hansel & Gretel*
17 *Slings and*
18 *Somewhere near in the dark*
19 *Holy Terror, come and get her*
20 *Saying body in the dark again*
21 *Forest*
22 *Wrapped in plastic*
24 *Dudley Road*
26 *Unhuried, the animal*
28 *Even so, a flowering*
30 *What won't*
32 *Like a pitcher of water*
33 *Where wolves were*
34 *Where wolves weren't*
35 *Running back again, recurring*
36 *Evelyn Tables*
39 *Can't not*

Undarling

There you are,
wanting what you want –

More beer in your glass?
　　　Fine.
A slim breeze? I can't promise,
　　　but okay.
An empty street? Anything, anything,
　　　just ask.

So you ask.

Sometimes you get what you're after,
and sometimes I'm sorry, but no,
you should try again later.

Later, door locked, your hands
dip below the surface of the
water and break at the wrist.

Your body
　　　and your body below
　　　　　　the water split

　　　like the stuttering
　　　break in paused video footage.

　　　Here, too, you are getting
　　　what you wanted, just by
　　　asking, though it doesn't
　　　seem like it.

Here, too, you are asking.

A slim breeze on an empty
street and anything,
 anything you want.

An arc, and etc.

Trying to be a good thing
twice – once for practice,
then once again for the
photograph.

Here, the stunned voices
of birds eat themselves
in the air, hollow and
eggshell thin, less sounds
than descriptions
of sounds.

The houses on either side
sit, swollen around the
middle like relatives
pushed away from the dinner
table, belts undone.

The porch light was left
on all night as a gift
to welcome us back,
but now, confettied with bugs,
it kept us outdoors, penned
into the darkness while
we worked up the nerve.

The road wasn't even a road
until the first house came
to pin it down. Unnamed, just
a way to move between small
towns, a rippled seam pulled

through the woods by an
unskilled hand.

I don't remember who took
the key, who moved first, who,
laughing, pulling their jacket
over their head, ran onto the porch
and fought with the decades-old lock.

I know that the door was opened,
eventually, just as I know that
later on, before stepping
into the shower, I shook my hair
over the sink and loosed
something with wings.

Versus

i
Ophelia in the shower
washing her hair with
unscented soap.

ii
Your impression
of the face I take
to parties is propped up
between the first time I burned
our breakfast and the final time
you offered to fix the smoke detector.

iii
I wrote notes in the steam
collected on the shower door,
meant as love poems,
they listed too far
towards mundane.

Buy milk, I wrote, meaning
don't stop. Remember your keys,
I wrote, meaning you are an
upper-cut above the rest.

Eggs, cheese, paper towels,
but I meant

my bath may be full of blood,
my hands muddy as grave-diggers'

but I taste every second of your tongue

and I miss every chamber
of your fictional heart

and I'd sink
every one of my battleships for you.

iv
I write pay the gas bill
and I mean
if only you would ask.

Hansel & Gretel

The road splits
like a tongue
in the distance.

On one side, the woods
and woods on the other.

The story starts this
way: a boy and his
sister, two little bodies,
breaking bread standing
at the kitchen table.

Somewhere in the house
a woman rises almost
to the top of her sleeping
but turns against her
husband, stays under.

Outside, the wind.
A forgotten line full of clothes
tenses, snaps, clean sheets
covering the garden in snow.

At some point the
brother's body will thicken
like a plot. The girl's eyes
will sound out small o's,
send out smoke signals
which stick in the rafters,
but those things are

still miles away
along a trail,
across a river,
and down a garden path.

First, there are crumbs.

The house where things
are finally starting
has been having bad dreams,
but it is damp, and it is
cold, and can't be made
to share.

Outside, the way
through the woods
is readying itself.

Tomorrow, perhaps,
a brittle little, battled
little double set
of feet will waver at its
edge, will set off
uncertainly
dropping
markers like x's,
like kisses,
like jewel

after jewel

after jewel.

Slings and

Say, We send them from bows,
they pierce us.

Say, The morning was deep
with its own good feeling.

Steady yourself. I was cruel
in my bluer days, short limbed
and singular in my desires.

You were a moveable target,
all teeth and lips, all tongue
and throat.

Say the airborne
arrow stalks us, singles us out,
what then?

There is a saint
in the hallway painting her face
in my mirror while I, in my burning,
have licked my bottom lip raw.

I chose, was chosen. Decided
where the path should go

but fell asleep, woke up run through,
the measure of my madness
an arrow, pointing at the trouble
it had caused.

Somewhere near in the dark

Something prized and bloodless
or chipped off and lost, rattling inside
like an uneven engine idling somewhere
near in the dark.

My brothers, returning to their
cities, wish me luck while I,
in turn, pretend I didn't hear
and watch the small dog, split
in the softness of her belly,
arch away from the grass,
cowed by a snap of pain

and then forgetting it, returning
to the task of searching over
the frosted lawn for something
she misplaced.

Holy terror, come and get her

It sometimes happens, and has happened
here, that the hero isn't the hero at all:

The hero is a knife, a paperback, or a street
after the parade has passed through –
something decorous, something dangerous.

For months, out of nowhere, the smell
of hyacinths seeping out of everything.

We pulled the paper from the walls,
put our food in airtight boxes, gave our
clothes to friends to wash and keep.
When it rained (and it rained), we opened
all the windows and doors, and hoped.

We stayed inside, one at a time, keeping
strict notes on every movement that
wasn't one of ours. The house
thrilled at our attention, heaved and settled,
chattered its teeth as the wind blew
through. We slept in our coats – for
warmth, at first, and then for fear
of being the last one inside, alone.

The morning of the final day, we ate.
We grinned. We spread our papers
on the living room floor and made a map,
made each other crowns, a rose, a ship.
We left a note. We left.

Saying body in the dark again

The body should be sewn together
with hair, hollows filled with cotton
and breadcrumbs and mulch. Clay eyes,
closed over, sticky fruit in the chest
for a heart, slivers of soap for lungs.

Let the ribs be a wicker basket,
the teeth be cubes of sugar, the
backbone a length of hose. Apples
in the cheeks and throat, a gently
folded paper tongue.

Soak the skin in milk until it softens,
then leave it on the curb to be taken away –
make the body like a bed, with sheets and
blankets pulled tight, turned down.

For each knuckle, a silver ring – one
you can stand to part with. Cover
the hands with foil to keep the heat
in. Consider all the angles. Pour
paint in through the mouth, let it
fill the carved-out veins and alleyways.

In the bowl of the head, arrange a handful
of ice so that it melts, slowly, into a pool
of clean water. When you're finished, admire
your neat work. Clear down your table. Rest.

Forest

If I tell you I dreamed a forest I'm lying, but listen.

I dreamed a forest with a feathered heart, a river piercing
through its northern flank. No animals, and then a shattering

and something springing, fully formed, onto four legs. In the high
branches, a coven of bees thicken the air with their urgent bodies.

I am lying, but kindly. I ate a forest of hair and rust, filling my pockets
with mud so you'd know where I'd been when I said I wouldn't be long.

The light in the forest was one hundred bulbs on the verge of pinging
back into dullness, just enough life left to see the film of darkness just

beyond. Under every surface, the generator-hum of insects. The path
carried on forward in spite of everything else, but lost its nerve, let itself

be rubbed out, then let itself be nothing. I have started a map, starting with me.
Then the trees. Then the river. Every inch says you are here, you were here,

you are here again. Then, when I get there, I'll start on the centre, that nest
of feathers and grass and fur.

The awning of branches and leaves keeps the weather out
for most of the year, but here in the middle there's a break,

a slight space carved out where something is trying to get through. It's not
blue sky – I dreamed a forest, but kindly – but it's deep, and it's there,

and that's true, near enough, for now.

Wrapped in plastic

As though you came already
ready-chalked at the edges,
ripe to be wrapped in plastic
and left in the woods, or
spooned out onto the sidewalk.

What could be lovelier
than winding up slippery
and split from edge to edge
so that someone you never met
can slowly, inch by scene by inch,
learn to be a different kind of man?

We understand you
might consider mourning
your blood – the tang of it
in the air, catching in the throat, your hair –
as it's sluiced from the gullies and traps
of a cool metal table, but stop. Think.

Who might,
right now, be rolling
his thumb around the lip
of his next drink, flashing back
to his wife, thin as paper and washed
blue: dead, or worse – a bitch.
You'll stand for something now,
so don't spoil or pucker, even when
they've hauled you, whole,
out of the water.

Don't bloat, or pout.
You're someone's daughter.
Someone might even say
"What if that was your daughter?"
and pin up a picture of your
most important self. You're
a point, well made.

You are obvious, the way a glass
smashed against a wall is obvious.
Even if someone stumbles over a sliver, nicks
their skin and bleeds a little, once
the glass is broken its only use is to remind us
of the moment that it broke.

Dudley Road

Summer rotted the mesh
on the windows and we didn't
sleep for sleeping too much,
a carved wooden boat of a bed
for my mother, and me on a
mattress in the next room.

Every room hung heavy
from its walls.

In the kitchen on the first night
the disposal kicked up sparks,
a special-occasion fork
sticking in the throat.

One morning, my mother
and grandmother woke early, watched
as twelve wild turkeys stammered
their way across the lawn.

I woke up after noon
to hear the story twice:

Ugly birds, heads loose
in a too-big morning;
chattering birds, making
their simple way along.

Lunches were held in laps,
picked up and eaten from paper
plates. It was too hot to stay

suspicious of the well-water,
too far from town.

Once, I'd thought
the rooms were honey-scented,
but now I trapped the smell of wax,
and dust, and the woods outside.

In one bedroom there was
the chalky skull of a deer resting
on the bed, bald and blithe, unmoved
for months.

My grandmother didn't climb
the stairs, slept in the living room
under the soft eye of the television,
the light from passing infomercials
casting back and forth across her.

The days before we left
for home, my mother unstuck
the dark wood furniture from its
twenty-year positions, swept and
polished and worried the vacuum into
reluctant, clattering life.

Every penny unearthed
was dutifully handed over to
her mother, who sulked and
seethed in the doorway, watching
to see that everything re-found
itself in the same exact place.

Unhurried, the animal

Snatched, the wound
where the hair had been
flashes red – quick panic,

then quieted. Even now, so
close to the end of yourself,
your body up to its old tricks
thickening the river, damming it.

The point of it all the insult pin-sharp
to mark where in the day it happened
the point of it all is missing,

then remembering,
the specialness of your body
spread like honey on a piece of glass
and hung around my neck.

Then, when my neck is finished with,
the charm will be passed on,
to someone who won't know
your hair lifting, briefly, as we stood
on the dim platform waiting for a train

which arrived, imperfectly,
right when we expected it.
They won't believe in the fact of you,

only
in the fact that I believed,
that I wanted to return to

the room of your body
but found that there was
no door, only a lock.

Even so, a flowering

Great, thick branches
grow into what you
thought would be
the light outside
your window.

You can still stand
with your coffee and
watch, say something
about birds and their
nearness, and almost
believe it, but the mornings
won't unfurl themselves
on your kitchen counters,
and when it comes, again,

to winter, you won't
be able to remember
yourself, still blotted
at the edges by sleep,
leaning your weight
over one hip, hair wet, letting
the light lick out, warming you
up to the day.

Even so,
a flowering, regular
and ripe.

Even so, a beach of shade
to come back to on rare

hot days. Let's not be too coy
about what giving in
might mean, what
else there is on offer.

But I should leave it
up to you. Take an axe.
Hire a man for the
weekend. Or move,
aim for somewhere
drier, where the ground
resists,

where mornings come in
greedy as weeds to cover
every inch of what
you own.

What won't

i
The slaughtering of light;
not now, but soon enough

ii
Seldom-used words for soft,
and body, and crown

iii
Beds in the warmest parts of the room

iv
An unclaimed coat,
the room still smelling of ash
and shoe leather

v
These sitting hands,
one on top of the other, waiting
and warm animals
        She said it was a mouse
got in and under and died,
billboarded with flies
in a closed room

vi
Horse teeth for luck

vii
Watching films where someone
stands at a sink and someone comes in
behind them, a hand to move their hips

or a knife to part their ribs

viii
The drained lake in the middle of the park,
something wanted until it wasn't

ix
The mud, the field,
the house full of guests.

Like a pitcher of water

Lowered by ropes
onto a bed made of ropes

waiting to be the next
thing in this list
of next things,
buttoned into panic
like a coat.

Where wolves were

Caught in the weave of your
why are you so nervous system
you might always find that you're
waiting to be called inside from the
yolk of light under the lamppost,
some rising voice saying your name,
saying it's only getting later, you'll
be sorry tomorrow.

And then, tomorrow. A different
lamppost, a different kerb, the
cars just too close to let you cross
safely for a while. You spy your
small chance, dip your toe into
the river, and then your heel.

On the opposite bank, long grass.
You hail a taxi; let it come for you,
then salt the ground behind you.

Where wolves weren't

Smaller and smaller mercies,
like a clear radio signal
all the way home, like your lights
being the only set banking across
the white front of your house as you
pull into your driveway in the dark.

Running back again, recurring

Madam, in Eden I'm Adam
but Eve was all that came before.
And before the fruit burst between
her crooked teeth and bled, I was
the beginning of the story,
the madman, Adam and all his ribs.

Never odd, or even,
or even after that; the morning
an upright miracle when her voice
was a bell and we were animal things
proving ourselves wild, wolves
in wolf's clothing.

No devil lived on
before the light, and her mouth,
became the old danger. I was
a box of bones, a man who
fell, was falling,
was full.

Evelyn Tables

Jars after rows of jars
of parts, turned inside
out or split through
the belly to show the
meat – the lungs, the throat,
a scooped out centre and
the thing that grew there,
        briefly.

On boards, a map
of nerves pasted into the
cherry-coloured wood. Couldn't
you see that in the middle
of our kitchen?
        I asked.

Couldn't you imagine
sitting down to breakfast with
some body's wiring under your knife
and fork? Delicious, you said,
and turned to look at the
collection of half-birds, hands
in your pockets like you were
afraid someone would take you
        at your wrists.

I asked, still blown
and dirty from the city,
too-thick tights, a wet wool coat,
if you could think about anything
other than teeth. Looking
into the cabinet, then

at our reflection in its
glass, you let your face pull
together, puzzled, saying
>	Teeth? What teeth?

There's hunger at the heart
of it, but before that there's
your jaw dropping open like
a purse. I asked you if you'd
come and see me if I was pickled
and put out in sections. You
pretended not to hear, moved
to the next display – blanched,
looked knocked. Make a joke,
>	I said, make me feel better.

A trophy case full of severed
pricks, a choir of them, a
gang, a peck. You moved,
mixed in with a group of
women looking miserably into
>	their itineraries.

Another plank of wood against
the wall, the branches of arteries
under varnish. Look, I said, a bed.
Couldn't you see it under the window
in our room? Wouldn't it be nice
to sleep and move over some memory
of a heart, at least? I fished a
hand out of your pocket, saying
let me, and you let me bring it
up and mime a nip, puppyish, trying.
I'd tear you into strips if I could
>	get close enough.

But for now
I swallowed the lump of hand
you'd offered, and followed you out
past the racks of scalpels, the
scaffolds of bones, the plucked
bodies treading water in their jars,
        watching us go.

Can't not

Can't not
and shouldn't ever,
but still, that lurching
softness interrupts
to ask if you've been
sleeping, offers
to fetch water
and whatever else,
waits and wades
through every

If I, then I, so I

in your arsenal
and still delivers,
tender-awkward,
in a box
just big enough
for itself and
a thin wrap of
tissue paper,
exactly what
you've missed.

Acknowledgements

'Undarling' and 'An arc, and etc.'
appeared on *The Cadaverine*, December 2012
'What won't' appeared in *Gigantic Sequins 3.2*,
'Versus' appeared in *Magma 52*

EYEWEAR PUBLISHING

EYEWEAR PAMPHLET SERIES
BEN STAINTON EDIBLES
MEL PRYOR DRAWN ON WATER
MICHAEL BROWN UNDERSONG
MATT HOWARD THE ORGAN BOX
RACHAEL M NICHOLAS SOMEWHERE NEAR IN THE DARK
BETH TICHBORNE HUNGRY FOR AIR
GALE BURNS OPAL EYE

EYEWEAR POETRY
MORGAN HARLOW MIDWEST RITUAL BURNING
KATE NOAKES CAPE TOWN
RICHARD LAMBERT NIGHT JOURNEY
SIMON JARVIS EIGHTEEN POEMS
ELSPETH SMITH DANGEROUS CAKES
CALEB KLACES BOTTLED AIR
GEORGE ELLIOTT CLARKE ILLICIT SONNETS
HANS VAN DE WAARSENBURG THE PAST IS NEVER DEAD
DAVID SHOOK OUR OBSIDIAN TONGUES
BARBARA MARSH TO THE BONEYARD
MARIELA GRIFFOR THE PSYCHIATRIST
DON SHARE UNION
SHEILA HILLIER HOTEL MOONMILK
FLOYD SKLOOT CLOSE READING
PENNY BOXALL SHIP OF THE LINE
MANDY KAHN MATH, HEAVEN, TIME
MARION MCCREADY TREE LANGUAGE
RUFO QUINTAVALLE WEATHER DERIVATIVES
SJ FOWLER THE ROTTWEILER'S GUIDE TO THE DOG OWNER
TEDI LÓPEZ MILLS DEATH ON RUA AUGUSTA
AGNIESZKA STUDZINSKA WHAT THINGS ARE
JEMMA BORG THE ILLUMINATED WORLD
KEIRAN GODDARD FOR THE CHORUS
COLETTE SENSIER SKINLESS

EYEWEAR PROSE
SUMIA SUKKAR THE BOY FROM ALEPPO WHO PAINTED THE WAR
ALFRED CORN MIRANDA'S BOOK

EYEWEAR LITERARY CRITICISM
MARK FORD THIS DIALOGUE OF ONE

Lightning Source UK Ltd.
Milton Keynes UK
UKOW07f1803281114

242373UK00001B/2/P

9 781908 998620